T0083049

JOHN PHILIP SOUSA

arr. Robert Gower

THE WASHINGTON POST MARCH

MUSIC DEPARTMENT

OXFORD
UNIVERSITY PRESS

To Gen. Frank Hatton and Mr Beriah Wilkins

The Washington Post March

JOHN PHILIP SOUSA
(1854–1932)
arr. Robert Gower

© Oxford University Press 2019

Printed in Great Britain

OXFORD UNIVERSITY PRESS, MUSIC DEPARTMENT, GREAT CLARENDON STREET, OXFORD OX2 6DP

The Moral Rights of the Composer have been asserted. Photocopying this copyright material is ILLEGAL.

20
1.
2.
mf
25
sostenuto
31
cresc.
37
1.
2.
mf

41
47
53
1.
2.
f
ff
58

Con larghezza
65
ff
72
78
1.
2.